Someone Who Listens
By Aaron Fields

Copyright © 2025 Aaron Fields. All rights reserved.

Published by The Write Perspective, LLC

All rights reserved. No part of this book shall be reproduced or transmitted in any form or by any means, electronic, mechanical, magnetic, photographic including photocopying, recording or by any information storage and retrieval system, without prior written permission of the publisher. No copyright liability is assumed with respect to the use of the information contained in this book. Even though every precaution has been taken in preparation for this book, the publisher/author assumes no responsibility for errors or omissions. Neither is any liability assumed for any damage that results from the use of the information in this book.

ISBN: 978-1953962-75-1

🌸 Remember: It's okay to be imperfect. Listening is enough. Staying near is healing.

Theme: Co-regulation, emotional safety, and naming feelings

**Feelings come and go. They don't stay forever.
Today, Milo feels….. a lot.**

Milo feels happy when Mama sings.

Milo feels frustrated when his block tower falls.

Mama kneels close.

"It's okay to be mad," she says. "I'm right here."

Milo feels better when Mama hugs him close.

Milo feels silly when he puts socks on his hands.

Milo feels unsure when it's time to say goodbye.

Mama holds his face gently.

"I'll come back," she says. "Your feelings are safe with Miss Johnson."

Milo feels shy when the room is loud.

Miss Johnson sits beside him.

"It's okay to stay quiet," she says. "I'm right here.

Milo feels excited when he builds a tower.

Milo feels sad when his tummy hurts.

Papa strokes Milo's back.

"It's okay to feel yucky. I'm not going anywhere."

Later, Milo feels calm again. His breath is slow and steady.

Feelings come and go. But someone always stays.

🧠 Notes for Adults

All behavior is communication. From infancy through early childhood, children express what they feel through sounds, movements, and big emotions. It's not our job to fix their feelings---- but to stay present and help them feel safe being human.

This story was created to model what co-regulation looks like in everyday moments: naming emotions, staying near, and offering calm when children can't find their own. Over time, your gentle presence becomes the foundation for your child's emotional resilience.

www.ingramcontent.com/pod-product-compliance
Lightning Source LLC
Chambersburg PA
CBHW041433040426
42450CB00022B/3477